WELCOME

to the

KINGDOM

Pastor Neil Gottman

ISBN 979-8-89526-149-1 (paperback)
ISBN 979-8-89526-150-7 (digital)

Christian Faith Publishing
832 Park Avenue
Meadville, PA 16335
www.christianfaithpublishing.com

Printed in the United States of America

CONTENTS

INTRODUCTION

Giving thanks unto the Father, which has made us to be
partakers of the inheritance of the saints in light; who
has delivered us from the power of darkness and hath
translated us into the kingdom of His dear Son.

—Colossians 1:12–14

Welcome to the kingdom!

God has always operated under a covenant. He made a covenant with Adam, Noah, and Abraham, which was passed to Isaac and Jacob. He made a covenant with Moses for the nation of Israel. But try to grasp this truth: The covenants are always unilateral, meaning God sets the conditions apart from man and they are all given to and through a single man. God has made a covenant for all mankind in and through His Son, our Savior, the Lord Jesus Christ. For those of us who have trusted the truth of the gospel and have received the declaration of justification from God, through the shed blood of Jesus, Paul here, in his letter to the Colossians, tells us to thank the Father for three things.

First, because we have been assured of an inheritance; second, because we are no longer under the gripping power of sin, which keeps us in darkness; and thirdly, we are often, even now, translated into the kingdom of Jesus. This is a spiritual kingdom that truly exists in the hearts of millions of believers. The kingdom is an everlasting kingdom, with an eternal king, King Jesus. In 1 Thessalonians 2:12, we are told that we were *called* into this kingdom. We are told, throughout the scriptures, the wonderful things that God has in store for the kingdom subjects. But just as it was in the Old Testament, when God called the Israelites out of Egypt to a promised land that flowed with milk and honey, there were conditions of obedience to receive the full blessings of the land. God told them they would drink from wells they had not dug and they would eat from vines and plants they had not planted. He told them there would be battles, but He would send an angel before them to assure their victory. There were ever so many wonderful things for them if only they would obey. However, upon reaching the entrance to this land and having sent in spies to spy out the land, they made a tragic decision based on their fleshly minds and emotions and were now destined to wander for forty years with nothing to eat but manna.

The kingdom of Christ has wonderful provisions for those who will follow the King and His commandments, principles, and precepts. There may be some real challenges but not without a way of escape. Our King loves His subjects and truly wants the best for them, but He also knows what we need by way of faith and grace, and He will always provide what He knows best. Paul went through so many difficulties on his journey in the kingdom, but Jesus gave him the strength and faith to see him through.

In this book, I believe God has commissioned me to make a true attempt in making a clear distinction between the kingdom and life of the kingdom to the life that most Christians know and are accustomed to in the organized, institutionalized, denominationalized, traditionalized church of today. Jesus did not call us to "go to church" but rather to "be the church."

When I meet with *church* people and ask the question, "What was Jesus's last command to His church?" Most of them have no idea at all, or they make a feeble attempt to talk about the Great Commission or some other pet argument or belief. However, the answer is very clear and quite revealing as it unfolds in practice or lack thereof.

> A new *commandment* I give unto you, that
> you love one another, even as I have loved you,

that you also love one another. By this all men shall know that you are My disciples, if you have love one to another. (John 13:34–35)

In order to see this clearly, we must ask the question, "Why is this a new commandment?" The answer is really very clear: Jesus was ready to usher in His kingdom. The command was to kingdom citizens. This particular command was directed specifically to kingdom people. During the evening, before His death, He reiterated His command several times.

The apostle John, near the end of this life, wrote the letters of 1, 2, and 3 John. In 1 John, he reminded us over and over again of his command and its consequences of disobedience. First John 2:8–11 reads,

> On the other hand, I am writing a new commandment to you, which is true in Him and in you, because *darkness* is passing away, and the *true Light* is already *shining*. The one who says he is the Light and yet hates his *brother* is in the darkness until now. The one who loves his brother abides in the Light and there is no cause for stumbling in him. But the one who hates his brother is in the darkness and walks in the darkness, and does not know where he is going because the darkness has blinded his eyes.

First John 3:10–19 and 22–23 reads,

> By this the *children of God* and the *children* of the devil are *obvious*: anyone who does not practice righteousness is not of God, nor the one who does not love his *brother*. For this is the *message* which you have heard from the beginning, that we should love one another; not as Cain, who was of the evil one and slew his brother.

And, for what reason did he slay him? Because his deeds were *evil*, and his brothers were righteous. Do not marvel brethren, if the world hates you. We know that we have passed out of *death* into *life* because we love the brethren. He who does not love, abides in death. Everyone who hates his brother is a murderer; and you know that no murderer has eternal life abiding in him. We know *love* by this, that He laid down His *life* for us; and we ought to lay down our lives for the brethren. But whosoever has the world's *goods* and beholds his brother in need and closes his *heart* against him, how does the love of God abide in him? Little children, let us not love with *word* or with *tongue* but in *deed* and truth. We shall *know* by this that we are of the truth and shall *assure* our heart before Him.

And whatever we *ask* we receive from Him, because we *keep His commandments* and do the things that are *pleasing* in His sight. This is His commandment that we *believe* in the *name* of His *Son* Jesus Christ, and *love* one another, just as He commanded us.

First John 4:7–12 and 20–21 reads,

Beloved, let us *love* one another, for *love* is of God; and everyone who loves is *born* of God and knows God. The one who does not love does not know God for God is love. By this the love of God was *manifested* in us, that God has sent His only *begotten Son* into the world so that we might *live* through Him. In this is love, not that we loved God, but He loved us and *sent* His Son to be the *propitiation* for our *sins*. Beloved, if God so loved us, we also ought to love one another. No one has beheld God at any time; if we love one another, God *abides* in us, and His love is perfected in us.

If someone says "I love God," and hates his *brother*, he is a lair for the one who does not love his brother whom he has seen, cannot love God whom he has not seen. And this *commandment* we have from Him, that the one who loves God should love his brother also.

As we work our way through this book, I pray that God will enable us to see the very real difference between church life and kingdom life. I have no intention of trying to show any dark or evil side to the organized church of today because I know after traveling in her ranks for over fifty years, there are many wonderful saints and well-meaning people on the rolls. The real attempt at this writing is to bring to light and the truth of God's plan for the kingdom, the church, the bride of Christ and to differentiate between what is of God and what is of man.

Paul wrote, "Beware least any man spoil you through philosophy and vain deceit, after the rudiments of the world, and not after Christ" (Colossians 2:8). I simply ask you to read and study with an open heart and mind, seeking only truth that will set you free.

CHAPTER 1

Called to Be Kingdom Saints

So that you may walk in a manner worthy of the God
who calls you into His own *kingdom* and *glory*.

—1 Thessalonians 2:12

What a wonderful privilege to know that God has invited me into His kingdom. The Greek word here translated "calls" is the word *kaleo*, meaning "to invite." God's invitation is out to all who will hear His voice and by faith accept the invitation to live and walk in this kingdom. This is a holy call from a holy God, and in our appreciation, we should desire to walk worthy of this holy God's calling. Our ticket, if you please, to enter this kingdom was very costly. It was the shed blood of Jesus Christ on a very cruel cross. To you and I, the ticket is free. We call it grace, but we must first reach out and receive it by faith. Having received this gift, hear what Colossians 1:13 says: "For He *delivered* us from the domain of *darkness* and *transferred* us to the *kingdom* of His *beloved son*."

We have been transferred into this kingdom, and we are now to be referred to as saints. Romans 1:7 says, "To all who are beloved of God in Rome, called as *saints*: Grace to you and *peace* from God our *Father* and the Lord Jesus Christ." First Corinthians 1:2 states, "To the *church* of God which is at Corinth, to those who have been *sanctified* in Christ Jesus, *saints* by calling, with all who in every place call upon the *name* of the Lord Jesus Christ, their Lord and ours."

The scripture is quite clear that we are now saints by calling. The Greek word for *saint*, according to the Greek Lexicon, is *hagios*, meaning "holy," "set apart," "sanctified," "consecrated," "chaste," "pure." Its fundamental idea is separation, consecration, and devotion to the service of deity, sharing in God's purity and abstaining from earth's defilement.

What changed? Everything changed. When I, by faith, received God's gift of grace and salvation, He created in me a new being and gave me His Holy Spirit to dwell there. He made me a saint, *by His definition*, and has translated me into His kingdom. It is now my privilege to live as a kingdom subject and to honor and obey my King, King Jesus.

How exciting and incredible is this! My King has promised to love me, protect me, and provide for me. And all He asks in return is for me to love, honor and obey Him. How could I not have "an attitude with gratitude?" You see, understanding the kingdom and kingdom life is much more than what we today attribute to church life. It is not just attending a gathering once or twice a week, singing a few songs, giving some money in the bag, shaking a few hands with a big phony smile on my face, and then going back to work all week. Kingdom life is 24-7. It is a new life in an old world. It is a calling from God to become salt and light in a rotting dark world. We are called to be preservative and to enhance quality of life in the world in which we live, but we are not a part of this world. We are to be a beacon of light to show this world the way to God and heaven and to dispel the darkness. If we would only look at this as a privilege and not a duty, it would change entire attitudes.

You might be saying now that you are not qualified for such a position or title, but you need to know that God has qualified you. Colossians 1:12 says, "*Giving thanks* to the Father, who has qualified us to *share* in the *inheritance* of the saints in the *Light*." Maybe I can help you by explaining some terms of scripture—*sanctification*, *justified*, and *justification*.

The word *justification* is a legal term that refers to a practice of making something right out of something wrong. God took the entire sin debt of the world—past, present and future—and He imputed that to His Son, Jesus Christ. To *impute* means to "give one's account." So God took your sin and my sin and all sin and transferred it to the account of Jesus. So now Jesus must pay the account in full. The payment God demands is holy pure blood. In Leviticus 17:11, it says, "For the life of the flesh, is in the blood, and I have given it to you upon the altar, to make atonement for your souls."

The flesh is the problem because of the sin nature of the flesh. The sin nature comes through the blood by a man, and it had to be a man that paid the price. But wait, the price is not just any blood. It had to be pure blood. Jesus was born of a virgin, and thus, the sin nature did not transfer to Him because He was from the Holy Spirit. His blood was pure from this sin nature, and God said it was satisfactory to satisfy the sin of every man that would come by faith and receive this justification. So now we who have come to Christ are justified in God's eyes by faith in the pure blood of Christ.

Having received justification, we now are set aside for God's glory—the term is *sanctified*. Sanctified is an action that God does, and in so doing, He calls us into a process of *sanctification*. This is a process of becoming holy. It is God's plan to make us like Jesus. For many of us, that is a hard struggle, but understand that you have been given the Holy Spirit to destroy the flesh and to bring life and immortality to our souls.

In Romans 8:10–17, we read:

> And, if Christ is in you, though the body is dead because of sin, yet the spirit is alive because of His righteousness. But, if the Spirit of Him, who raised Jesus from the dead, dwells in you, He who raised Christ from the dead will also give life to your *mortal* bodies through His Spirit, who indwells in you. So then brethren, we are under obligation, not to the flesh, to live according to the flesh, for if you are living according to the flesh, you must die; but if by the Spirit, you are putting to death the deeds of the body,

you will live. For all, who are being led by the Spirit of God, are sons of God. For you have not received a spirit of slavery leading to fear again, but you have received a spirit of adoption as sons by which we cry out "Abba! Father!" The Spirit Himself bears witness with our spirit that we are children of God and if children, heirs also heirs of God and fellow heirs with Christ, if indeed we suffer with Him, in order that we may also be glorified with Him.

Now think deeply about that scripture. We are heirs to the kingdom. We are saints by the very declaration of God and called to His kingdom to live as saints, not sinners. You see, the kingdom is already here in the hearts and lives of those of us that are saved through the new birth. This kingdom has no earthly name such as Baptist, Methodist, Catholic, or any other name given by man. All such things are man-made and divisive. God has no such plan. In scripture, we see the church at Ephesus and the church at Thessalonica—the churches that meet in various named homes. The word *church* is simply meaning "the called-out ones." All are kingdom subjects with only one king, King Jesus. He is the head of His body, the church. Please take note that He is not just a figurehead but the Head. He has all authority in heaven and earth.

Life in the kingdom is clearly outlined in the scripture for us to follow. Love is our commandment, and making disciples is our commission. Second Corinthians 5:18–20 states,

God, who reconciled us to Himself through Christ and gave us the ministry of reconciliation, namely, that God was in Christ reconciling the world to Himself, not counting their trespasses against him, and He has committed to us the word of reconciliation. Therefore, we are ambassadors for Christ."

We are ambassadors for Christ to carry the gospel and to make disciples—certainly not a burden but rather a privilege.

While we are on this journey, we find that serving others is our freedom. Galatians 5:13 says, "For you were called to freedom brethren; only *do not turn* your freedom into an opportunity for the flesh, but through love, serve one another." When you and I truly learn to die to my wishes, my desires, my needs, my wants and to put others first, we will live free. The hardest enemy to drive out of our lives is the *me-ites*. May God give us grace and strength to not always think about us and ours.

CHAPTER 2

Camelot

There is a mythological story written many years ago of an English king named Arthur. King Arthur was a very strong and courageous king, with a heart for a life of peace and prosperity for his subjects. He lived in a world that was very hostile toward that way of thinking. The world around him, as it is today, had a mindset to conquer or be conquered. There could be little, if any, cooperation for the betterment of mankind. King Arthur had built a large city called Camelot. This was a city of light, a city where its inhabitants could enjoy the life that the king had envisioned. If you could look for the word *Camelot* in the dictionary, it will tell you it was a "time, a place or atmosphere of idyllic happiness." It sounds sort of like a city described in the Book of Revelation.

But you see, Arthur had an archenemy who wanted badly to destroy both him and his city and would stop at nothing to do so. Consequently, Arthur needed an army to protect and defend his kingdom, and he had called a small group of men to be the front guard for his city and his way of life. They were very elite, dedicated, and loyal men and would forever be known as the knights of the roundtable. Camelot was *more* than a place. It was a vision, a conviction to die for, a way of life to truly be desired.

Brother to brother, shoulder to shoulder, back to back—we will battle to protect and promote Camelot.

At the center of Camelot was the roundtable of King Arthur and his knights. At this table, there was no distinction of rank or importance. It was this round table that gave strength and adhesiveness to this entire way of life.

As the knights were seated, they would lay their swords on the table, pointing directly to the center, where there was an inscription that gave life to their vision: "In serving each other, we live free." No self-preservation, no self-interest, no self-promotion, only others. No class distinction, no racial or monetary distinction, only others. And of course, without even a notice, we find others serving us.

This entire idea of serving others and living a life of caring and servitude is exactly the life that Jesus both taught and lived. He told us that when we lived out this life, we would show the world that we were His followers. He sets the standard, and He sets the example in His own life and has commanded us to follow that pattern. He even gave us the powerful person of the Holy Spirit to enable us to do exactly that. But we have another power within us that does not want to give in to this idea. This enemy within us is jealous and protective of itself and does not want to surrender.

We find then that surrender is not the real answer. Only death will give us the full measure of Camelot life. Kingdom life is possible once the old self, the old nature, is crucified but not until.

Romans 8:5–13 reads,

> For those who are according to the flesh set their *minds* on the things of the *flesh*, but those who are according to the *Spirit*, the things of the Spirit. For the mind set on the *flesh* is *death*, but the mind set on the Spirit is *life* and *peace*, because the mind set on the *flesh* is *hostile* toward God; for it does not *subject* itself to the *law* of God, for it is not even able to do so; and those who are in the flesh cannot please God. However, you are not in the flesh but in the Spirit, if indeed the *Spirit* of God *dwells* in you. But, if anyone does not have the Spirit of Christ, he does not belong to

Him. If Christ is in you, though the *body* is dead because of sin, yet the *Spirit* is alive because of *righteousness*. But, if the Spirit of Him who raised Jesus from the dead *dwells* in you, He who raised Christ Jesus from the dead will also *give life* to your *mortal* bodies through His Spirit who dwells in you. So then brethren, we are *under obligation*, not to the flesh, to *live* according to the flesh— for if you are living according to the flesh, you must die; but if by the Spirit, you are putting to death the *deeds* of the body, you will live.

Colossians 3:5–10 reads,

> Therefore, consider the members of your earthly body dead to *immorality, impurity, passion, evil desire* and *greed* which amounts to *idolatry*. For it is because of these things that the *wrath* of God will come upon the sons of disobedience, and in them you also once walked, when you were *living* in them. But, now you also, put them all aside: anger, wrath, malice, slander and abusive speech from the mouth. Do not lie to one another, since you laid aside the old *self* with its evil *practices*, and have put on the *new* self who is being *renewed* to a true *knowledge* according to the *image* of the One who created him.

In Romans 8:5–7, we clearly see the enemy within. It is the carnal mind. It is the mindset to always guard self and to always satisfy self. But in the soul of the man, there is also a free will—a choice that can choose between right and wrong, good and evil. It is only when the choice is made for good that the power of God through the Spirit will come to the battlefront to secure our choice. In verse 13, it is clear that the Spirit can and will put to death this enemy called the flesh.

In Colossians 3:5, we are told to "put to death" fornication, uncleanness, inordinate affections, evil desires and covertness. The tenth commandment says, "Thou shall not covet thy neighbors' house; thou shall not covet thy neighbors' wife, nor his man-servant, nor his maidservant, nor his ox, nor his ass, nor *anything* that is thy neighbors'."

We live in a world that tries to continually play on our covetness, always portraying something *better*, something *nicer*, something giving the flesh *more pleasure*.

True "kingdom life" is attainable for anyone willing to make the choice for the death of self. God will always make a way and will always give us what we really need, and then He will give us more in order that we might share. Sharing and giving and loving and caring are basic in real kingdom life. What we give and what we share will always return to us in good measure.

CHAPTER 3

Institutionalized

We know from human experience that more often than not, when you put someone into an institution, such as a prison, they can develop a psychological barrier that keeps them from living outside the institution in any other normal or functional way.

All one has to do today is look with honest and open eyes and thinking and realize that the church (particularly the church in the Western culture) has become institutionalized. Every organized church today is like a cookie-cutter church, with much the same patterns and habits. Our order of service is virtually the same—our pastors, elders, bishops, and boards. They all represent the pattern of the world's corporate structure. Our traditions have become so familiar and frozen that we function like robots oftentimes, not even realizing what we are doing. We sing songs and read scripture with our spirits so traditionalized that we are not able to actually see and hear the truth.

Let me give you an example. At Christmastime, we always sing the hymn "Joy to the World," which has not one single word pertaining to the birth of Christ. This hymn was written concerning the second coming of Christ and the curse being removed from the earth. When I point this out to even pastors and worship leaders, it is like smoke from a bottle that just floats away in the breeze, and we continue to sing this song at Christmas having no idea at all what the message really is.

Many preachers today believe and teach that we are the representation of the Laodicean church of Revelation, and yet we tend to not hear what Jesus said to the church. We go on doing the same things because we are institutionalized, and we cannot break the cycle. Jesus said that we are to "anoint our eye with eye salve that we might see."

If we would give an honest evaluation to our traditional church of today, we would be compelled to say that there is little, if any, room for the Holy Spirit to actually lead in our gatherings. There is little, if any, room for the gifts of the body to function, and we trod on saying what a great service we've had.

This matter that we are discussing has robbed us of our freedom in Christ. In Galatians 5:1, we read, "Stand fast, therefore, in the liberty with which Christ has made us free and be not entangled again with the yolk of bondage." We are living in continual bondage to traditionalism, denominationalism, and institutionalism that has blinded us and bound us with ropes of our own making. I am not at all saying that every tradition is bad. I simply want us to see that kingdom life is not found in these things.

There is a better way. This way could be summed up in this saying: "In serving others, we live free." Galatians 5:13 states, "For brethren, we have been called unto liberty; only use not liberty as an occasion to the flesh (serving of one's self) but by love, serve one another."

True kingdom life is about one another, with Jesus as the head. I pray you will see even more clearly as you read the chapter on "Intentional Community." In that chapter, we will make a real effort to give a true biblical insight into God's plan for the church. We can make a feeble attempt to rationalize our institutionalism by arguing growth and cultural changes we have experienced, but I believe all these are invalid and only show our ties to our institutionalized ways.

If God wanted us to have a certain order of service, doesn't it seem logical that He would have given us that order? In the Old Testament, when God gave the instructions and the plans for the tabernacle, He clearly outlined not only the design but also the order in which things were to be done. He gave very detailed instructions concerning the way each offering and sacrifice were to be conducted.

It certainly seems reasonable to me that if there was to be a set order of service, God would certainly have shown us that order. This certainly makes for the strong argument that there is a freedom given to us to allow the Holy Spirit to live and work and move within our corporate body that might be far different than our set "order of service," to give us a "word of knowledge," a "word of wisdom," "psalm," or a prophetic utterance to challenge us.

Any such occurrence in the institutionalized order of service would certainly be deemed "out of order."

If the argument is that our churches have grown so large—that without the order of service, there would be chaos—I agree. My answer is that we need to get smaller to get bigger. What is our goal? Is our goal to grow numbers or to grow individuals into the likeness of Christ? Why did Jesus concentrate so much of His time and effort on just twelve men? He reached out to the masses, but He focused on the twelve. This, in itself, should give us a clue into God's plan.

I challenge you to look beyond the order of things today in the church where you attend and try to see the real plan of God for His people to become. Christ is and sees the freedom that He has given us to allow the Holy Spirit to work in corporate structure.

As born-again children of God, we know that we have the Holy Spirit of God living in our bodies. First Corinthians 6:19 reads, "Know ye not that your body is the temple of the Holy Spirit, who is in you, whom ye have God." In 1 Corinthians 2:12, it says, "Now we have received, not the spirit of the world, but the Spirit, who is from God, so that we might know the things freely given to us by God." John 16:13 reads, "Nevertheless, when He, the Spirit of truth is come, He will guide you into all truth."

I believe that most Christians believe this, but few know how to truly receive instruction from the spirit of God. Many have knowledge but no revelation. First Corinthians 2:14 says, "But the natural man receives not the things of the Spirit of God, for they are foolishness unto him; neither can he know them, because they are spiritually discerned."

Let's take a look at just how all this functions in real life. First, we must understand how we are made and how each part functions.

It is clear from scripture that God has created us a three-part being. We are body, soul, and spirit. Understand that the body is earthly as it was created from dirt. The Bible says that God created man in His own image (a spirit) after His own likeness (three in one). Now we have a spirit in a body, but then God breathed life into His creation, and he became a living soul. Hebrews 4:12 speaks of the dividing of the soul and the spirit. Prayerfully, we can now try to see how all this works together by understanding how each part works.

The body basically relates to its five senses. We see, feel, hear, taste, or smell; and our body responds by sending impulses to our brain, which is the major functioning component of our soul. Our soul is divided into three major functioning parts—the intellect (the way we think), the emotion (the way we feel), and the will (where we make choices). Then we have the spirit. It is here that the spirit of God dwells, and it is where we sense the voice of God, in that still, small voice. It is in the spirit of man where our conscience is active. It is like our stop light that says to us, "That is wrong," "Stop," "Don't go that way," "Don't do that," etc. Also, we now have a quickened intuition saying to us as our green light, "This is the way. Walk in it." And certainly, we have in our spirit the communion factor, where we worship God only in spirit and in truth.

So now we see that the body responds to senses, the soul responds to feelings and rationale, while the *spirit responds to truth.* Our challenge is to realize the battle going on in our own body will respond to either our *feelings* and *rationale* or the *truth of God* and *His Word.* In our soul is that free will that gives us the ability to choose. We are given the spirit to lead us into all truth, and so our choice is always between our feelings and rationale and truth. This is the great battle that rages in each us. This battle is clearly defined in Galatians 5:17–26, which reads,

> For the flesh *sets its desire* against the Spirit,
> and the Spirit against the flesh; for these are in
> opposition to one another, so that you may not
> do the things that you please. But if you are led
> by the Spirit, you are not under the Law. Now the

deeds of the flesh are *evident*, which are: *immoral-ity, impurity, sensuality, idolatry, sorcery, enmities, strife, jealousy, outbursts of anger, disputes, dissen-sions, fractions, envying, drunkenness, carousing,* and things like these, of which I forewarn you just as I have forewarned you, that those who *practice* such things shall *not inherit* the *kingdom* of God. But the fruit of the Spirit is *love, joy, peace, kindness, goodness, faithfulness, gentleness, self-control;* against such things there is no law. Now those who belong to Christ Jesus, *have crucified the flesh* with its *passions* and *desires*. If we live by the Spirit, let us also walk by the Spirit. Let us not become boastful, challenging one another, envying one another.

Please take careful note of verse 21, where we receive the warning that those who follow the flesh and its impulses and emotions shall not inherit the kingdom of God. The remedy is found in verses 22–26.

The crucifixion of the flesh is offering it up to God on our part and the Spirit giving new life that comes from God. The great struggle for Jesus ended when He prayed in the garden and said, "Not my will, but thine be done." He gave up His attachment to this world in every way.

We are in the world, but we are not of this world. We must set our affections on things above and not on things of this world. We must have the mind of Christ.

In our institutionalized frame of mind, we are afraid to allow the Holy Spirit to take us out of the box for fear of chaos breaking out. It does seem to me that on the day of Pentecost, there may have been some chaos as the world would see it, but in the chaos, there were three thousand souls saved. Am I suggesting that there be no order in our services? Not at all am I suggesting that. However, I do believe there needs to be more of an awareness of the Spirit moving, and we can adapt to God's plan. I was very young in the Lord but was not yet locked in to a particular order of things.

I was preaching for two weeks in a tent revival in a very small community. It seems as though not much was being accomplished for the kingdom. It was on a Saturday night, and the tent was filling up to standing room, which would only be about three hundred to three hundred fifty people. There was a lady attending that night from a local Christian college, and she was at the piano to sing a song to open the services. She began to sing the song "If That Isn't Love." I suddenly realized that something was different, and I felt prompted to do something different. As she was finishing the song, I took a folding chair from the platform and set it on the grass right in front of the platform. I then took the microphone and simply told the people that this was our prayer chair and that if there was anyone who needed prayer or if they had a sin burden and wanted us to pray for them, they should come sit in the chair. I then asked for anyone who wanted to pray for that person to come. I hadn't even finished yet when a man, about halfway back, jumped up and came to the front. He took the microphone and began to confess his sin; he wept and pleaded for help. The people quickly responded and came to pray for him. As they began to retreat to their seats, another person came to confess and ask for prayer. One by one, for the space of two or three hours, people were praying for one another, and before the night was over, many people had prayed to receive the Lord.

In church lingo of today, we always have a time of "praise and worship." By a very simple definition, *praise* is our response to all of God's mighty works while *worship* is acknowledging God for who and what He is. The scripture says that God "inhabits the praises of His people." With that being the point of truth, when we truly praise God and He inhabits our praises, worship will be normal, Spirit-filled Christian response. Will that happen in fifteen or twenty or forty minutes, or will it happen at all?

It certainly is my prayer that as we learn to live our true kingdom life, we find the freedom given us in Christ to truly follow the Spirit and not the clock and not some rigid order that must be adhered to.

CHAPTER 4

Presupposition

I want to deal with the matter of presuppositions and how it can affect the church. There are numerous reasons that we all are prone to developing presuppositions, but it primarily comes as a result of traditions. We begin to assume that things are as they are or that we are to do or not do certain things because we do not know another way. Our parents did it this way, as well as grandparents, so it must be right. Oh, how deceived we can be! We sometimes go to the Word of God to try to prove our position, not to find the truth.

I want to start with the matter of prayer. We hear something like this on a regular occasion: "Let's begin with a word of prayer." Please tell me, what is "a word" of prayer? Now if we need to pray, let us pray, but please see that this is generally only tradition, and we have presupposed that this is the thing we are to do. Oh, we Christians certainly pray a lot—at every meal, for elections, for our government, and the list goes on. We pray a lot. My question is, Are we really praying from a burden or a true heart of gratitude, or are we just doing it from a religious mindset that presupposes that we are to do that? I know that by now, you have begun to think that somehow, I am not in favor of prayer, and nothing could be further from the truth.

Jesus told us to "pray without ceasing," meaning to me that we are to pray about everything. He did tell us to pray for our enemies, our fellow believers, our leaders, and our sick. He told us to pray for our needs day by day, but we all know that much of our praying is done out of tradition, not out of true burden.

Any presupposition that is truly God-honoring must originate in truth and truth as found in God's Word. To presuppose that something is right or wrong, merely based on past and tradition, is very wrong and dangerous. In the church world of today, we are so shallow, and so few really know the depths of God's Word. We read, but we do not study. We hear, but we do not understand because the truth of God must come by discernment and revelation. We do not have the receptor to receive it. If you were in total darkness and someone struck a match many miles away, you, no doubt, could see the light *if* you had the proper receptor. Our physical eyes are simply not made to see that great distance.

The Holy Spirit that lives in a true Christian's body is the receptor to see and reveal the truth and to let us understand the deeper things of God. Once truth has been revealed, it is no longer presupposition, but it is life and light to live by. It is the entrance into our entire way of life and the establishment of a way of holiness here on earth.

Moses prayed the right prayer in Exodus 33:13: "If I have found grace in Thy sight, show me now Thy way that I may know Thee." To know His way is to know Him, and His way is a way of Holiness. In Hebrews 12:14, we find, "Follow peace with all men, and holiness, without which no man shall see the Lord."

Oftentimes when we must make a decision for our actions in life, we simply follow our presuppositions because we do not know the Word of God. We have not ingested His Word into our hearts and minds, so we make some decision that seems logical to us. Logic comes from the mind and often is based on the way of the world, not the truth of God's Word. For you and I truly to live out this "kingdom life," we must learn of the ways of the King. God's Word gives us instruction and direction for nearly everything in life. He deals with everything from marriage and child-rearing to business principles. He gives us clear instructions for interpersonal relationship and resolving conflict. He gives us advice on dietary and health issues and certainly makes a case for a good work ethic. He warns us about becoming entangled in the world system and says clearly, "Love not the world, nor the things of the world."

If we would spend just half as much time in His Word as we do on the TV and our computers and phones, we would soon begin to develop an entirely different way of life. When we go to His Word, we must not just read, but we need to study and dig out the complete truth. May I, at this point, remind you that there is a day of reckoning, and we must all stand before the judgment seat of Christ to answer for those things done in our body, whether good or bad. If we go through life only living on our presuppositions, we are likely to be very sad on that day of reckoning. We might even find that we are not even in the Lamb's Book of Life. What a tragedy to have some false religious notion that you are okay with God and end up in hell. The warning is clear in Matthew 7:21–23:

> Not everyone who says to Me "Lord, Lord," will enter the kingdom of heaven, but he who does the will of My Father, who is in heaven *will enter*. Many will say to Me on that day, "Lord, Lord, did we not prophesy in Your name, and in Your name cast out demons, and in Your name perform many miracles?" And then I will declare unto them, I never knew you; *depart from ME, you who practice lawlessness.*

Economic, political, and social morals change with generational and cultural changes, but the truth of God's Word never changes. Kingdom life is for kingdom subjects that are truly "born again" by the Spirit of God and can only be fully enjoyed when we live it by His principles and directions.

Seek His way that you might know Him.

CHAPTER 5

Re-Digging Old Wells

In Genesis 26, we find the story of Isaac who is about to face a major crisis. He has been ordered by King Abimelach, king of the Philistines, to move with all his people and herds to the Valley of Gerar. Many years before, his father, Abraham, had dwelled there and had dug numerous wells of water. These wells had since been stopped by Philistines after Abraham's death.

Isaac now has a real crisis because of their need for water, both for the people and the herds. I suppose there were a number of things Isaac could have done, like calling for water diviners to find new water or form a committee of experts in the field of locating new water supplies. Isaac chose rather to re-dig the old wells of his father where he knew there was ample water.

Today, in our crisis, in the kingdom, we really don't need new and experimental things; we simply need to go back to the things we know work. These things are made very clear in scripture if we are willing to dig them out. We must re-dig the old wells. As we progress, through this work, we hope to shed light on some of the things that worked in the beginning of the kingdom and brought them freshwater.

You might want to say to me now, "Where is the crisis?" In the church today, we see a divorce rate that is as high as or possibly higher than we see in the world. We see young people and families backing out of the institutional church by droves and simply looking for truth and the real, corporate Christ in the true body, yet so few are able to find it.

We see new churches popping up by the masses, all claiming to have the answers, but they continue to simply be a cookie cutter of the only pattern they have seen in the world. They simply offer different decorations or icing.

We continue to seek our 501 (c)(3) from the government, so we can get our tax-free status. We ask the government if we can be a church, and we beg for our discount everywhere because, I guess, we simply forget that God is greater than all the governments of the world and can readily supply our needs with no discount needed.

We think we are rich and increased with goods, but Jesus knows we are poor, naked, and blind. We are truly the church of Laodicea.

While we argue and split in all our denominational and often insignificant differences, the world is taking people on a path that surely leads to eternal damnation.

But not only is the world to blame because we, as the church, are so desperate to build our ranks so we can build our programs and buildings. We water down the truth of the gospel and fill our rolls with lost but hopeful people—without repentance, without fruit, without true, life-altering change in lives that continue to go the way of the world.

When did God change? When did He withdraw His holy demands? When did He change His programs for the church, so He could fit cultural morals of the day?

Please don't turn me off here, but read on and let the spirit of God speak to your heart and mind. We can get back on track. It's not too late to believe God for better things.

Let's take a real look at some things that are very clear in God's Word and ask God to guide us and deliver us from the world, the flesh, and the devil.

The Apostles' Doctrine

One of the wells that needs to be re-dug is the apostles' doctrine. In Acts 2:41–47, it reads

> So then, those who had *received* His Word were baptized; and that day there were added about three thousand souls. They were continually *devoting* themselves to the *apostles' teaching* and to the *fellowship*, to *breaking* of bread and to *prayer*. Everyone kept feeling a sense of *awe*; and many *wonders* and *signs* were taking place through the apostles. And all those who had believed were together, and had all things in *common*; and they *began* selling their property and possessions and were sharing them with all, as anyone might have need. Day by day, continuing with one mind, in the *temple*, and *breaking* bread from house to house, they were taking their meals together with *gladness* and sincerity of heart, *praising God*, and having favor with the people. And the *Lord* was adding to their *number* day by day, those who were being saved.

The apostles' doctrine, I believe, is the only real place to begin as we re-dig old wells. This is really where it all started, and I might add, started with great success. This scripture starts with, "They that gladly received His Word," and ends with, "The Lord added to the church daily." We must learn to not only hear the Word of God but to actually receive it and internalize it. That means we will begin to live it out by faith and practice, and by way of simple observation, people will be drawn to the truth—Jesus Christ.

So what was this "apostles' doctrine?" I suppose by simple deduction, we must know that the only doctrine or teaching they knew was what they learned from Jesus. We then might observe that what they were teaching was now being lived out by the people's fellowship, breaking of bread, prayer, a singleness of heart and purpose, and oh yes, meeting one another's needs.

The apostles' teaching and/or doctrine, no doubt, was very positive and strong concerning the resurrection of Jesus and the power of God that brought this about.

In John 20:19–22, we see the disciples after the crucifixion.

> When, therefore, it was evening, on that day, the first day of the week, and when the doors were shut where the *disciples* were, *for fear of the Jews*, Jesus came and stood in their midst, and said to them, "Peace be with you." And, when He said this, He showed them both His hands and His side. The disciples, therefore, rejoiced when they saw the Lord. Jesus, therefore, said to them again, "Peace be with you; as the Father has *sent* Me, I also send you." And, when He had said this, He breathed on them and said to them, "Receive the Holy Spirit."

In verse 19, they were hiding away for "fear of the Jews." Now on the evening of the resurrection, Jesus visited them and did something that forever changed, not only them but the entire course of history. He breathed on them and gave them the Holy Spirit. The indwelling presence of the Spirit was now going to produce in them His fruit of love, joy, peace, patience, kindness, goodness, faithfulness, gentleness, and self-control. They had been promised this when Jesus assured them that He would not "leave them comfortless." It was here—no doubt—that they, having the indwelling of the Spirit, began developing a whole new relationship of loving and caring. In Acts 2, we read, "On the day of Pentecost, they were all with one accord in one place."

It was now time for the Spirit that indwelled them to be manifested to the world. With the sound of a mighty wind and cloven tongues of fire, they were filled and empowered with a boldness to witness to the world the truth of a risen Christ. Their faith had become embolden beyond measure. They were now ready to meet the challenges the world would confront them with.

In Acts 3 and 4, we see the story of the healing of the lame man and the persecution that followed, but the disciples remained strong and undivided because of one great truth: the *resurrection*! They now had become so knit together of one heart and one mind that they truly performed as one.

It was now that the wonderful things that they had learned from Jesus began to be taught and practiced. The teaching ministry of Jesus really began as recorded in Matthew 5 to 7, commonly known as the Sermon on the Mount. We find, first of all, in the beatitudes His teaching about the attitude and characteristics of a true disciple. The poor in spirit are those who came with absolutely nothing to offer the kingdom, except total and complete surrender and death to self. They tend to mourn over their sin and the sin of those around them, but they are strong in their faith. They have insatiable hunger and thirst for God's righteousness in their personal lives, but they still show mercy and pureness of heart toward others, always looking to make peace.

As a result of life filled with the grace and glory of God, persecution will be a very real thing to be expected, it should be faced with joy and gladness because we know they are a part of God's wonderful kingdom plan. In 2 Timothy 2:11–12, we read, "It is a faithful saying: for if we be dead with Him, we shall also live with Him; if we suffer, we shall also reign with Him." Here we can see that the cross always comes before the crown. This is never pleasant to the flesh, but it needs to be a joy to the Spirit. His promise is sure that the crown will be worth many crosses.

Through the remainder of chapters 5 to 7, Jesus teaches us many things that are to be a part of the kingdom life. He speaks to us about salt and light and our need to portray these qualities to the world. He teaches us about getting along and making reconciliation with one another. He speaks about lust, adultery, and divorce (which, by the way, is as prevalent in the church as in the world).

He says that our word should be our bond, and we should even love and respect our enemies. He comes down hard on outward religious practices to impress others. He teaches us about prayers and forgiveness, and He makes a very clear statement about our lust for money and things. "No man can serve two masters… You cannot serve both God and money" (Matthew 6:24).

After giving these priorities and principles of kingdom life, Jesus spent the next many months with His disciples living out what He had just taught them. He simply became a living testimony to the possibilities of true kingdom life lived out in a dark and sinful world.

Having given the message and living the testimony, He now comes to the last week of His life on earth. And knowing His time with His disciples is now coming to an end, He gathers them together not just for the last supper but to give them last-minute instructions and encouragement.

The beloved apostle, John, gives us a very detailed account of the last night together in the Gospel of John, chapters 12 to 17, from which we can draw a clear picture of the Lord's heart as He washes His disciples' feet and announces His departure.

In this very intimate setting, Jesus truly shows His heart of a servant as He girds Himself with the towel, pours water into the basin, and kneels to wash their feet. Just imagine, here is the great Creator, the God of the universe, the great Healer and Giver of life, humbling Himself and giving comfort and service to those whom He loves. The example He gives us here is twofold. First of all, the act of this foot washing is to those chosen and close to His heart. He is not washing the feet of the world but only those in very close and intimate proximity of His fellowship. Second, He shows us that there is no "leader" or "special individual" who is exempt from servanthood, but rather, the truth that whoever is a true servant is also a true leader.

In chapter 13, verse 33, Jesus declares His going away, and in verses 34–35, He gives them (and us) His last commandment: "A *new* commandment I give unto you, that you love one another as I have loved you and that you also love one another. *By this* shall all men know that you are my disciples, if you have love, one to another."

Two things should stand out to us in these verses. First, why is it new? Second, the intimacy that is to be displayed to show the world the true love (*agape*) that can come only from God. If we have spiritual eyes to see and ears to hear, we realize the newness of this commandment is because Jesus is introducing a whole new plan—though not really new because it has been before the foundation of the world. But now He is about to begin the bringing together of His body, His bride, the chosen ones, the called-out ones, the *ecclesia*. The command is to this special group coming together as one to display to the world the true love of Christ.

This body of Spirit-filled believers now has a commandment and a plan for true world evangelization. In Acts 2:41–47, we see the true evangelistic plan of God being fulfilled as the Lord adds to the church (ecclesia/called-out ones) daily those who should be saved. As the corporate Christ is displayed through the love and concern of the body for one another, the lost take note and are drawn in by this love. It's not about going door to door, passing out tracts, or holding special meetings; it's about living out the Christ life as one.

What we called the great commission is not a command but a directive to share the good news of Jesus Christ. We can share this good news to all of those who question life of oneness that we live because of the hope that is within us through Jesus Christ our Lord.

The apostles' doctrine is readily available for us to study once we realize the simple truths that they only had what Jesus taught them both in word and example and they truly were now passing it onto the church.

Once again, "beware lest any man spoil you through philosophy or vain deceit, after the tradition of men, after the rudiments of the world and not after Christ" (Colossians 2:8).

"Oneness"

Another well to be re-dug, where we find living water, is the doctrine of oneness. It becomes clear that this was being taught to the first church. In Acts 2:44, they "were together and had all things common," and in verse 46, they were of "one accord and singleness of heart." In chapter 4, verse 22, they were "of one heart and one soul."

The doctrine of oneness begins in Genesis 1 with the name of God, *Elohim*. This is a plural noun in form but is singular in meaning. Elohim is further confirmed as plural when Elohim said in 1:26, "Let Us make man in Our image." Throughout scripture, we see plurality of God and yet only one God in substance. Three in one trinity—Father, Son and Holy Spirit—yet only one God. This is one of the cardinal doctrines of scripture from the earliest records. We do not understand or even comprehend the possibility or reality of this because of the finiteness of our human logic and reason. However, for those who truly have the spirit of Christ, we know in our spirit the truth of this doctrine.

When God made the woman from the rib of the man in Genesis 2, Adam said, "They shall be one flesh." The apostle Paul wrote to us in Ephesians 5:28–33 concerning Christ and His church and used the metaphor of husband and wife as one flesh. Again, we are not able to put scientific explanation for this, but we receive it by faith as truth.

All this being said, I ask, Why is it so hard to understand or accept the oneness of the body of Christ and to see the necessity of the corporate manifestation of the same?

God has put into the body of Christ a plan and a purpose for each of us to fulfill. Do we not understand that we are interdependent, relying on one another?

This really is not a private matter but rather a corporate necessity for proper function of a healthy body. The apostle Paul, once again, makes a clear case for this in 1 Corinthians 12 and 14. Over and over again, reference is made to the oneness of the body, and yet we go on trying to function on our own or in some denomination or religious setting with no regard for others. In our Western culture, for sure we have developed an independent nature that is filled with pride and fear of rejection that keeps us from truly developing any real intimate relationships. We will speak of this again in the chapter on "Intentional Community."

The oneness doctrine seems to be an area of darkness in the church that needs desperately to be uncovered and brought to light. I urge you as a reader to go to your Bible and search out this truth and let the Holy Spirit shed light on your understanding of this wonderful teaching. I believe, if we look carefully, we will clearly see that this doctrine was surely being taught by the apostles to the first church. It is only when sin and pride enter into the picture that we are drawn away from this truth. We need desperately to hear what God tells us in Ephesians 4:1–6:

> Therefore, I the prisoner of the Lord, beseech you that you walk worthy of the vocation, to which you are called with all lowliness and meekness, with long-suffering, forbearing one another in love, endeavoring to keep the unity of the Spirit in the bond of peace. There is *one* body and *one* Spirit, even as you are called in *one* hope of your calling; *one* Lord, *one* faith, and *one* baptism, *one* God and Father of *all*, who is above *all* and through *all* and in you *all*.

We are not to display our independence but rather surrender to our interdependence. The vineyard of God is as large as the world, and we know the fruit of the vine grows in clusters. The clusters can be many or few, but one truth remains: It is only when the clusters are crushed and blended together as one that the new wine comes forth.

Oneness is a blending of personalities. True oneness must contain tolerance, respect, and concern, with openness to the differences contained in personalities. Personalities are, to a large degree, inherent but are shaped by cultural and associational living conditions. We can learn from our associations to either appreciate differences or be closed to them with a rigidity that makes oneness nearly impossible.

We know, through much sociological experience and study, that there are only four basic personalities. If you were to establish a project of most any sort and blend these four, you would see something like this. Number one personality would say, "We need to dive right in and get this project on the road. There may be some challenges along the way, but we will deal with them as we come to them." The second personality would say, "I am all for this, and I believe we can make this a really fun-packed project, and everyone will truly enjoy this." The third personality will say, "I simply want to be able to do my part, just put me where I can be most helpful." The fourth personality will say, "I like the project. However, we must double-check every move and cross our *T*s and dot our *I*s."

Now when these four are blended together in an atmosphere of love, tolerance, and acceptance, you would have the perfect team for oneness.

The project laid out for us as Christians is to become as Christ is. The book of Ephesians makes this quite clear. The thing that continually blocks this is the lack of understanding and the intolerance of differing personalities. The cure for this is a surrender of your personality to Jesus Christ and a respect and admiration of each personality and person that is in Christ. We must come to the complete understanding that it is not about me and my thoughts and ways but about Christ and His thoughts and ways. His way is oneness—a blending of lives and a plurality of personality, all surrendered to Him.

CHAPTER 6

Living in Two Worlds

I believe it is important that we have a clear understanding and firm grasp on the truth that as a child of God, we live in two very distinct and different worlds at the same time. In this truth, we must also understand that we are subject to the laws, both physical and spiritual, at the same time. However, as we will find, there is one of these that takes precedence over the other in every area of our life.

The first of these, for the sake of this study, we will call "the world," and the other, we will refer to as "the kingdom."

The world was created by God, both in the physical as well as in an environmental way. When God had finished the physical creation, He gave man a plan. First, God planted a garden eastward. This fact, in itself, bears some thought and deep mediation. You see, God made Adam from the dust of the earth He had created, and then He planted a garden in the earth to bring forth the substance that man would need for physical life. Next, He put Adam in the garden "to till it and to keep it." It would seem that this was to be a pleasurable and gratifying experience. God, as well as Adam and Eve, was no doubt very pleased with this arrangement. He would come in the cool of the day and walk with them through this beautiful garden. Adam and his mate had all the provisions for life in a created world. I can only imagine how wonderful it must have been.

Just as it is with us today, when things seem to be so good and easy, we find ourselves wanting more and more, and it is not enough to just walk with God and watch Him provide. We soon try to take matters into our own hands and become our own god, going beyond what God has so freely given us. Sin happens! Our world falls into darkness and decay and is now subject to and destined to destruction.

Adam's world is now diminished to earning his sustenance by the sweat of his brow and be plagued by thorns and thistles. Adam's world is now subject to trials, bloodshed, sorrow, and grief, and the ultimate end is death.

This world is the world that you and I have to live in and be subject to all of its trials, sorrows, and pain. This world is filled with cultural and environmental challenges that demand our subjection. Our flesh nature, which is filled with sin and self, constantly is drawn by what the world now has to offer. Oh, the dilemma we are in.

But wait, there is another kingdom. This is a kingdom of truth, love, and light, and it is eternal. This kingdom is not subject to the world and its morals but is a superior kingdom that is here now for my and your living and joy. In this kingdom, there is love, joy, and peace for all who will abide by the King's word. Now understand that His word is law and is truth. It is meant for our good and our pleasure.

When standing before Pontius Pilate, Jesus was asked this question: "Art thou a King?" Jesus answered, "Thou sayest that I am a King. To this end was I born and for this cause, came I into the world, that I should bear witness unto the truth. Everyone that is of the truth heareth my voice" (John 18:37). It was then that Pilate asked the question that must be answered in each of our lives: "What is truth?"

Some years ago, I was teaching Bible class to the older students in a Christian high school, and I gave them a project to complete. I asked them to draw a symbol that to them best represented truth. When the papers were turned in, there were a number of crosses, Bibles, and other religious symbols. After some discussion on the matter, I went to the board and said I would draw my symbols. I simply placed a dot on the board like a period at the end of a sentence. To me, truth is like a period, it is the end of the matter, period. It does not change with time or conditions. Psalm 117:3 says, "The truth of the Lord endures forever." Jesus said things like "the truth will make you free" (John 8:32); "I am the Way, the Truth and the Life" (John 14:6); "The Spirit of truth will guide you unto all truth" (John 16:13).

The kingdom is a kingdom of truth established in the hearts of believers by grace through faith. It began in John 20:21 on the evening of the resurrection, when Jesus came to His disciples and breathed on them and said, "Receive ye the Holy Spirit." It is the Holy Spirit dwelling in the bodies of believers that brings communion and commonality to the kingdom. The kingdom was then released and manifested to the world on the day of Pentecost.

This kingdom came into a world of chaos and division, of sin and debauchery of every sort, but this kingdom began to knit men's hearts together as followers of Jesus Christ. They were filled with a power to stand against the other world and to come together in love and concern for one another. There was a true sense of community among those early believers. They sensed a new kingdom, that seemed to rise up within them and knit them together. It was not just a bunch of individual believers gathering together once a week but a body actually caring, feeling, and filled with anticipation and ready to reach out to one another in need. They became bold in their witness to the religious crowd and to the world at large because they truly believed in a risen Lord and were filled with the assurance of His presence to lead them and meet their need.

Who Is the King?

In kingdom life, it is so important that we get the right perspective on lordship and headship. Putting it in very simple terms, we can say that lordship is an individual matter while headship is looking to the corporate body of Christ.

We get our first insight into lordship in Genesis chapters 1 through 3. In Genesis chapter 1, we find the first name given to deity is Elohim. This name is used thirty-one times in this chapter, dealing with the creation. Elohim said, Elohim saw, and Elohim created. Having our first insight into the Creator and His creation, when we come to chapter 2, verse 4, we find the name given to deity is now Jehovah Elohim. This name is "Lord God." Surely, we must see from this that creation comes before lordship. If there were no creation, there would be nothing to be lord over. We also see in verse 16 of chapter 2 that the Lord God commanded. He lay down the ground rules, if you please.

In chapter 3, we first see the devil called the serpent, and he simply refers to his Creator as Elohim, acknowledging His existence and knowing His name but refusing by choice to call Him Lord. "Yea, hath Elohim said?" Likewise, the woman in verse 3 follows suite as she speaks of Elohim as being that exists and she is very aware of, but once again, she refuses to call Him Lord.

It seems evident that through this, we can come to some logical truth that will be applicable to each of us. First, we can see that there must be a creation by Elohim to give Him something to be lord over, and having created, He is Lord and has the right and authority to command. Second, we can see that even though He has created and has commanded, He still gives His creation a choice. We can also see, if we read on, that the wrong choice has dire consequences.

Lordship is an individual matter for each of us, and it is really all about obedience. If He is Lord of my life, it will be evident through my obedience to His commands. His last command before returning to His Father was for us to "love one another, as He loved us," and "He has given Himself for us." *Loving is giving*; giving always relates to others. I think it is important to say that we dare not think that "giving" is necessarily "loving." We can give without loving, but we cannot love without giving.

This now brings us to headship of His body called the church. Headship is indeed a corporate matter and is spoken of in verses like Colossians 1:8: "And, He is the head of the body, the church." The church is the body of Christ, made up of many members called the *ecclesia* or the called-out ones. This corporate body is indeed made up of all who have been made new creations in Christ.

Having been born again of the spirit of God and having received that same spirit into our bodies, we become a single part of this glorious body. However, this body is made as the fruit of the vine in clusters. There are large and small clusters, and all are important to the overall mission of God. As this mission is being carried out, God will crush each cluster together to make the new wine come forth. It is only when we yield to His hand and hear His voice that He now is truly head, not just figurehead. First comes lordship, then comes headship. We must learn to let Jesus Christ make the decisions in both our private life and our corporate life. Let Him crush us together with the clusters we are in to bring out the new wine for the world to see. May it be so.

CHAPTER 7

Abundant Life

Kingdom life is meant to be a life that is filled with an abundance of love, joy, peace, and all of the other fruits of the Spirit. Jesus said in John 10:10, "I came that they may have life (eternal salvation), and have it abundantly."

Particularly in our Western culture, we tend to relate that to finances and things that are tangible; but Jesus was talking about a life of faith and trust in Him to meet all our needs—physical, emotional, and spiritual—that we might find real contentment.

In order for me to illustrate this life, I want to take a look into the Old Testament for a *type* of this life and its possibilities.

In the book of Exodus, we find the children of Israel, God's chosen people, living in captivity to the Egyptians. In a study of typology, we see Egypt as a type of the world system we live in before we are saved. Pharaoh is a type of the devil who operates that world system. Because of our sin nature, we are held captive by its laws, tradition, and philosophies.

Their release from this slave situation would have to be miraculous, so God sent a deliverer in the person of Moses to lead them out. After Moses came, he met great opposition from Pharaoh. God then began to direct Moses to warn Pharaoh of the pending judgment by way of certain plaques.

The final plaque was that the firstborn of every household would die in one night. God then gave Moses exact instructions on how they could be delivered. It was a deliverance by the blood of a lamb. The people received these instructions very well and thus were delivered.

The same is true today for anyone who will trust God's promise of deliverance from the world system and their sin by simply trusting in the shed blood of Jesus Christ, the Lamb of God, for our deliverance. Turn your back on the world and all that it stands for. Trust in Jesus for your salvation, and you will inherit eternal life and will become "kingdom subjects." Colossians 1:13 says, "For He rescued us from the domain of darkness, and transferred us to the Kingdom of His beloved Son."

Is that all there is? Does God have more for us here and now as kingdom subjects?

Once again, go back to Exodus. God brought His people out of captivity from Egypt (type of world) and was now ready to lead them to a land of promise and provision for their time remaining on this earth. He began to give Moses His plan to take them into the land and how He would provide for them. He brought them out, and now He wanted to bring them in. Deuteronomy 6:23 states, "He brought us out from there in order to bring us in, to give us the land which He had sworn to our fathers."

The same is true for you and me today. Once again, Jesus said, "I have come that you might have life," but this is just the beginning. Our salvation is the starting point, and our journey begins in the wilderness, where we desperately need leadership and direction. God told the Israelites in Exodus 23:20–33,

> Behold, I am going to send an angel before
> you to guard you along the way and to bring you
> into the place which I have prepared. Be on your
> guard before him and obey his voice, do not be
> rebellious toward him, for he will not pardon your
> transgression, since My name is in him. But, if you
> truly obey his voice and do all that I say, then I will
> be an enemy of your enemies and an adversary
> to your adversaries. For My angel will go before

you and bring you in to the land of the Amorites, the Hittites, the Perizzites, the Canaanites, the Hivites and the Jebusites; and I will completely destroy them. You shall not worship their gods, nor serve them, nor do according to their deeds; but you shall utterly overthrow them and break their *sacred* pillars in pieces. But, you shall serve the Lord your God, and He will bless your bread, and your water; and I will remove sickness from your midst. There shall be no one miscarrying or barren in your land; I will fulfill the number of your days. I will send My terror ahead of you, and throw into confusion all the people among whom you come, and I will make all your enemies turn *their* backs on you. I will send hornets ahead of you so that you will drive out the Hivites, the Canaanites and the Hittites before you. I will not drive them out before you in a single year, that the land may not become desolate and the beasts of the field become too numerous for you. I will drive them out before you little by little, until you become fruitful and take possession of the land. I will fix your boundary, from the Red Sea, to the sea of the Philistines, and from the wilderness to the River *Euphrates*, for I will deliver the inhabitants of the land into your hand and you will drive them out before you. You shall make no covenant with them or with their gods. They shall not live in your land, because they will make you sin against Me, for if you serve their gods, it will surely be a snare to you.

Deuteronomy 8:6–10 states,

Therefore, you shall keep the commandments, of the Lord your God, to walk in His ways and to fear Him. For the Lord your God is bringing you into a good land, a land of brooks of water, of fountains and springs, flowing forth in valleys and hills; a land of wheat and barley, of vines and fig trees and pomegranates, a land of olive oil and honey; a land where you will eat food without scarcity, in which you will not lack anything: a land whose stones are iron, and out of whose hills you can dig cooper. When you have eaten and are satisfied, you shall bless the Lord your God, for the good land which He has given you.

God has promised to meet their every need and even more. This is the abundant life. Jesus has promised us that if we trust Him and walk by faith, He will make every provision for us. Philippians 4:19 says, "And, my God will supply all your needs according to His riches in glory in Christ Jesus."

When the children of Israel reached the point of entry to the promised land, we see the people's failure in Numbers 13:1 to 14:10.

The Lord spoke to Moses saying, send out for yourself men so that they may spy out the land of Canaan, which I am going to give to the sons of Israel; you shall send a man from each of their fathers' tribes, every one a leader among them. So Moses sent them from the wilderness of Paran at the command of the Lord, all of them, men who were heads of the sons of Israel. These then were their names: from the tribe of Reuben, Shammua, the son of Zaccur; from the tribe of Simeon, Shaphat, the son of Hori; from the tribe of Judah, Caleb the son of Jephunneh; from the tribe of Issachar, Igal the son of Joseph; from the tribe of Ephraim, Hoshea the son of Nun; from the tribe of Benjamin, Palti the son of

Raphu; from the tribe of Zebulun, Gaddiel son of Sodi; from the tribe of Joseph, from the tribe of Manaseh, Gaddi son of Susi; from the tribe of Dan, Ammiel the son of Gemalli; from the tribe of Asher, Sethur the son of Michael; from the tribe of Naphtali, Nahbi the son of Vophsi; from the tribe of Gad, the son of Machi. These are the names of the men whom Moses sent to spy out the land; but Moses called Hoshea the son of Nun, Joshua. When Moses sent them to spy out the land of Canaan, he said to them, "go up there into the Negev; then go up into the hill country. See what the land is like, and whether the people who live in it are strong or weak, whether they are few or many. How is the land in which they live, it is good or bad? And how are the cities in which they live, are they like open camps or with fortifications? How is the land, is it fat or lean? Are there trees in it or not? Make an effort then to get some of the fruit of the land." Now the time was the time of the first ripe grapes.

So they went up and spied out the land from the wilderness of Zin as far as Rehob, at Lebo-hamath. When they had gone up into the Negev, they came to Hebron where Ahiman, Sheshai and Talmai, the descendants of Anak were. (Now Hebron was built seven years before Zoan in Egypt.)

Then they came to the valley of Eshcol and from there cut down a branch with a single cluster of grapes; and they carried it on a pole between two men with some of the pomegranates and the figs. That place was called the valley of Eshcol, because the cluster which the sons of Israel cut down from there.

When they returned from spying out the land, at the end of forty days, they proceeded to come to Moses and Aaron and to all the congregation of the sons of Israel in the wilderness of Paran, at Kadesh; and they brought back word to them and to all the congregation and showed them the fruit of the land. Thus they told him, and said, "We went in to the land where you sent us; and it certainly does flow with milk and honey, and this is its fruit. Nevertheless, the people who live in the land are strong, and the cities are fortified and very large; and moreover, we saw the descendants of Anak there. Amalek is living in the land of the Negev and the Hittites and the Jebusites and the Amorites are living in the hill country, and the Canaanites are living by the sea and by the side of the Jordan."

Then Caleb quieted the people before Moses and said, "We should by all means go up and take possession of it, for we will surely overcome it." But the men who had gone up with him said, "We are not able to go up against the people, for they are too strong for us." So they gave out to the sons of Israel a bad report of the land which they had spied out, saying, "The land through which we have gone in spying it out, is a land that devours its inhabitants and all the people whom we saw in it are men of great size. There, also, we saw the Nephilm (the sons of Anak are part of the Nephilm), and we became like grasshoppers in our own sight, and so we were in their sight."

Then all of the congregation lifted up their voices and cried, and the people wept that night. All the sons of Israel grumbled against Moses and Aaron; and the whole congregation said to them,

"Would that we had died in the land of Egypt! Or would that we had died in this wilderness! Why is the Lord bringing us into this land, to fall by the sword? Our wives and our little ones will become plunder; would it not be better for us to return to Egypt?" So they said to one another, "Let us appoint a leader and return to Egypt."

Then Moses and Aaron fell on their faces in the presence of all the assembly of the congregation of the sons of Israel. Joshua the son of Nun and Caleb the son of Jephunneh, of those who had spied out the land, tore their clothes; and they spoke to all the congregation of the sons of Israel saying, "The land which we passed through to spy out is an exceedingly good land. If the Lord is pleased with us, then He will bring us into this land and give it to us—a land which flows with milk and honey. Only do not rebel against the Lord; and do not fear the people of the land, for they will be our prey. Their protection has been removed from them, and the Lord is with us; do not fear them." But all the congregation said to stone them with stones. Then the glory of the Lord appeared in the tent of meeting to all the sons of Israel.

Because of their unbelief and simple lack of faith, they could never experience the full measure of God's goodness and provisions.

The challenge that lies before each of us, as believers, is just the same as in the story of the Israelites. We too must learn to walk by faith in every area of our lives. We must believe God's word that He will meet our every need, not our want.

The abundant life available to us today is not a life without its challenges. Sometimes, the walls seem way to high, and the enemy far too big, so we fail to press on to God's intended purpose. We still must war with the enemies set before us, but God promised deliverance if we will trust Him and obey His Word.

This abundant life that Jesus came to give us is truly a life of peace and contentment. God has a simple plan for each of us and will give us all that we need to complete that plan. We are all given different gifts and talents, and when we use those to the glory of God and the fulfillment of His plan, He has promised to make every provision for our life.

Just like the Israelites, we too have the promise of God to live here and now in His Promised Land of safety and ample provision. Remember that "whatever is not of faith is sin" (Romans 14:23). Again, "Welcome to the kingdom!"

CHAPTER 8

Intentional Community True Kingdom Life!

I was raised on a dairy farm in Northeast Missouri. I grew up as a part of multigeneration family. We were a hard working family of three generations, working for the common good of all. My grandfather was one of seven brothers all living and farming their farms in one general locality. Because of the challenging times, during and immediately after World War II, we were a very interdependent community. It was not generally by choice but from necessity that we had a community life. I suppose you could call this "unintentional community."

When it was time for the various harvest activities, we would come together with our teams of horses and mules and eventually a few tractors to help one another gather harvest. We only had one machine for the various needs, and it would travel from farm to farm to reap the harvest. In the wintertime, we would go from farm to farm for the butchering of hogs for our years' meat supply. We had only one set of tools for this work, and they belonged to nobody but were available to everybody. Those were some wonderful times as we gathered together as families and talked and joked as we worked together. The meals were always something to behold, both at harvest and butchering times. As unintentional as it was, it worked very well, and everybody benefitted.

When God planned the kingdom for His Son, He called out people from all walks of life, called them the church (the ecclesia/called-out ones), put His Spirit within them, and said we were to love one another and become community. He gave us all differing gifts and talents, all of which are to be used for the common good. He basically said to us, "Now you folks get along and help one another" (bad paraphrase).

God made us relational. We need others even though we think many times we don't. Our culture has evolved into a culture of independence. Now remember that Satan is the ruler of this world, and it is apparent that he has brought about this evolution of independence. He will do and has done everything in his power to thwart the plan of God. We must see this and return to God's intended plan of community.

In today's church, we seem to lean in the direction of bigger is better. Now I agree that we need to bring the gospel to as many as will hear and then disciple them as our Lord has commissioned us to do. However, I believe that in order to truly get bigger and win more to Jesus Christ, we need to get smaller. How many does it take to form a community, and what would that look like?

I think the answer to these questions must begin with this statement: "Communion must precede community." There must be the building of trusting relationships to have community as I believe God has intended. These trust relationships are generally found in small units or families. In order for this to happen in a true Christian atmosphere, everyone must "die daily" and be devoted to a person not a project. That person must only be Jesus Christ. There must be vulnerability and openness, and when that is there, you will find true freedom.

The apostle Paul wrote, "For brethren, you have been called unto liberty, only use not liberty as an occasion to the flesh, but by love, serve one another" (Galatians 5:13). Die to self and serve others. Doesn't this sound a lot like Jesus?

Now what would that look like? I think that might be best answered through certain goals for intentional community.

Goal number 1 should be to show the world a complete picture of Jesus Christ through the body. The apostle Paul wrote,

> Unto me, who am less than the least of all saints, is this grace given, that I should preach among the Gentiles, the unsearchable riches of Christ and to make all men see what is the *fellowship of the Mystery* which from the beginning of the ages hath been hidden in God, who created all things by Jesus Christ. (Ephesians 3:8–9)

The key here is the "fellowship of the mystery." The great mystery that Paul speaks about was simply that the God of the universe would move His residency from the temple and the Holy of holies into the bodies of living saints, thus creating a fellowship with each saint being a particular part of the whole. He goes on to say,

> To the intent that now, unto the principalities and powers in heavenly places, might be known by the church (ecclesia, called out ones) the manifold wisdom of God, according to the eternal purpose which He proposed in Christ Jesus, our Lord. (Ephesians 3:10–11)

The true manifestation of God's wonderful plan is seen in the church, the corporate body of Christ. However, we don't seem to be doing very well in many areas.

Number 1: We have severed the body so badly and have become so divided by denomination, color or race, and in many cases, have truly done great harm to the cause of Christ with our division. Now we may argue our points of reason for such action, but the fact remains that there is still only one body of Christ and has no name but Jesus.

Number 2: We have structured most of our fellowships after the pattern of the world's corporate structure, and in the world's eye, we are hard to distinguish from the world. We build huge edifices that are rivaling in the world's structures, and we place at the head a man or men that become powerful and wealthy and even famous by the world's standards.

Could I, for a moment, give another scenario or possibility? Imagine a city with forty thousand practicing Christians that are divided into a hundred churches, each with buildings, staff, etc. Between all of these churches, the expenses of buildings, salaries, activities, and all the other various expenses run into unbelievable amounts of money.

Now let's break that down into small house churches of approximately fifteen people each—no salaries, no buildings, only the expense of renting a stadium or very large facilities for citywide worship. We actually create an atmosphere of relationships that can truly model the Christ we serve, and the millions of dollars of savings can become mission projects that go far beyond the church model of today.

Oh, I know that now many of you have turned me off as some idealist or radical anti-church person, but this is not so at all. What I just described so poorly was actually the picture of the early New Testament church. It really did seem to work pretty well for them— from house to house and then in the temple. How well are we doing at "loving one another" as Christ loved us?

This leads to goal number 2: being obedient to the last commandment of Christ given in John 13:34–35. There is no doubt in my mind that it is much easier to love someone you know, like family or very close relationship, than it is to love someone you don't know or maybe only know their name. By developing small families of believers into intentional community, the world will see the body manifesting itself in loving, caring, sharing relationships. Without the intimate small community setting, you may know someone's name and a few details about them but never really know them. How about a church in every single neighborhood?

Goal number 3 is the "perfecting of the saints." Once again, we find God speaking to us through the apostle Paul:

> And, He gave some apostles; and some
> prophets; and some evangelists; and some pastors

> and teachers; *for* the perfecting of saints, *for* the
> work of ministry, *for* the edifying of the body of
> Christ. (Ephesians 4:11–12)

God has given gifted men and women to the body with a purpose in mind. The purpose is to mature the saints spiritually so that they can serve the body by using the spiritual gifts God has given them. Thus, the result is the growth of the body of Christ into a oneness of Christlikeness. Our problem here is that we have come to believe that pastors, evangelists, teachers, prophets, and apostles are some very elite group that must become professionally trained to do the job and then thrust into some full-time, well-paying, professional role. Is it not possible that a pastor or a teacher can be used in a very small group or community setting as effectively as in some large group of people where very little, if any, community takes place? You see, community is about communion. Without communion, there is no community. In true Christian community, Jesus Christ must be the common denominator that draws us together in ministry and services with Christ as the focus.

Paul tells us in verses 13 and 14 of Ephesians 4 that the true potential is the unity of faith because we know (intimately) Jesus Christ and that we can become mature in our faith that keep us from being swayed away from the truth by those with evil intentions thus causing us to fall.

Goal number 4 is to supply the needs of the body, both spiritually and physically.

Please try to understand and grasp this truth: God's plan for the body, the church, the community of believers is a plan of interdependency—no lone rangers. Just like the physical body is interdependent and relies on various parts working together to maximize health and vitality, so is the body of Christ. The *New American Translation* reads like this:

> We are to grow up in all aspects to Him,
> who is the head, even Christ, from whom the
> whole body being fitted and held together by

that which *every* joint supplied, according to the *proper working of each individual part*, causes the growth of the body for the building up of itself in love. (Ephesians 4:15–16)

Every joint and every part are important to the growth of the body, and the need is for each part to work properly.

On the spiritual level, God has given numerous gifts that are to be used in this growth process. There are twenty-plus gifts listed in the New Testament. Most people that I know would say, "I don't know what my gift is so how can I use it?" The answer to that statement and question is really very simple: "Surrender yourself into the hands of God, and ask Him to use you and live your life by faith that He will guide your steps." Not everyone is called to preach or teach, but we are all called to service. Please stop here and read Romans 12:1–13.

What about physical needs? It is rather obvious what the practice of the earliest church was. They saw to it that no one was without. They practiced a form of communal life that was a life of total surrender of God's money, property, all for the supply of all. They trusted the apostles and later the deacons to channel the gifts to the right places. A careful reading and study of the New Testament makes it clear that we have a special obligation to fellow believers.

Again, in Ephesians, Paul wrote a very telling word, "Let him that stole, steal no more, but rather, let him labor, working with his hands the thing which is good, that he may have to give him that has needs" (Ephesians 4:28). Work and earn in order to supply the needs of others. James really put it on the line when he wrote,

What doth it profit, my brethren, though a man says he has faith and have not works? Can faith save him? If a brother or sister be naked and destitute of daily food, and one of you say unto them, depart in peace and be ye warmed and filled; notwithstanding, you give them not those things which are needful to the body, what doth it profit? (James 2:14–16)

Paul wrote to Timothy giving this admonition: "If any provides not for his own, and especially for those of his own house, he hath denied the faith, and is worse than an infidel" (1 Timothy 5:8). In the body of Christ, it seems very consistent with God's plan that we see to it that everyone's needs are met—needs, not wants. How can that best be accomplished without some taking advantages of our generosity and care? It can best be administered through small house churches, cell groups, care groups, and so on. In true intentional community, these needs will be recognized and met.

In 2 Corinthians 8, a careful reading will show us that it is first about a ready mind to be a supply line and that it is not about equal giving but rather equal sacrifice.

In true Christian community, in real kingdom life, there must be accountability both to Christ the King and to one another. "Am I my brother's keeper?" And the answer is yes!

The entire New Testament—book by book, chapter by chapter, verse by verse—unfolds a plan for kingdom life. We are shown how to encourage, admonish, counsel, and always love the brethren. We are to hold one another accountable and constantly encourage one another to live as Christ lived. We are to make sure that true needs, both spiritually and physically, are met by the body. We must learn to love one another through true service and caring for each other.

I am reminded of a story I heard about a little girl that was afraid of the dark. Every night, her father would put her to bed and pray with her after tucking her in. But night after night, she would soon begin to cry for her father, and when he came, she would tell him that she was afraid of the dark. Night after night, the father would assure her that Jesus was there with her and would watch over her. After several nights of this same scenario, as the father was about to leave the room again, the little girl said, "I know Jesus is here, but sometimes I need someone with skin on." Don't we all need this at times?

I believe that what I am suggesting in this writing will take some radical thinking and radical action on our part. Most will probably not heed the warnings of the impending dangers ahead and will continue on their independent ways; however, for those who see the truth and will surrender their independence and come together in small interdependent families, they will surely benefit and be greatly rewarded by the Lord.

Forming intentional community can happen in any church body. Just consider the idea and find one or two others to start and meet together and let the Holy Spirit give you direction.

May we each continue in the grace and mercy of our Lord Jesus Christ.

CHAPTER 9

Compromise

The word *compromise* is a word that should not be a part of the born-again Christian life. *Compromise* means "to settle for something less that what is required or desired."

In the story of the dialogue between Moses and Pharoah, we find that Pharoah was willing to compromise three times.

The first is found in Exodus 8:25–29, which reads,

> Then Pharoah called for Moses and Aaron, and said, "Go, sacrifice to your God in the land." And Moses said, "It is not right to do so, for we would be sacrificing the abomination of the Egyptians to the Lord our God. If we sacrifice the abomination of the Egyptians before their eyes, then will they not stone us? We will go three days' journey into the wilderness and sacrifice to the Lord our God as He will command us." So Pharoah said, "I will let you go, that you may sacrifice to the Lord your God in the wilderness; only you shall not go very far away. Intercede for me." Then Moses said, "Indeed I am going out from you, and I will entreat the Lord, that the swarms *of flies* may depart tomorrow from Pharoah, from his servants, and from his people.

But let Pharoah not deal deceitfully anymore in not letting the people go to sacrifice to the Lord."

"You can go but not too far. Stay where I can find you."

The world would say today, "It's okay to have your church service, but just don't go too far away and separate yourself completely from our control. We will give you a 501(c)(3) corporate structure 'because you asked us if you could be a church,' and we can still control your activity. We can also tax you and your employees and call it social security." They believe they can tax God. "Just don't go too far. Remember we are watching."

The second compromise Pharoah offered is found in Exodus 10:8–11, which reads,

> So Moses and Aaron were brought again to Pharoah, and he said to them "Go, serve the Lord your God. Who *are* the ones that are going?" And Moses said, "We will go with our young and our old; with our sons and daughters, with our flocks and our herds we will go, for we must hold a feast to the Lord." Then he said to them, "The Lord had better be with you when I let you and your little ones go! Beware, for evil is ahead of you. Not so! Go now, you *who are* men, and serve the Lord, for that is what you desired." And they were driven out from Pharoah's presence.

It is okay to go as men. Just leave your family and your worldly goods for us to keep you coming back. This was a compromise that he knew they could not accept.

The final compromise was in Exodus 10:24–28, which states,

> Then Pharoah called to Moses and said, "Go, serve the Lord; only let your flocks and your herds be kept back. Let your little ones also go with you." But Moses said, "You must also give

us sacrifices and burnet offerings, that we may sacrifice to the Lord our God. Our livestock also shall go with us; not a hoof shall be left behind. For we must take some of them to serve the Lord our God, and even we do not know with what we must serve the Lord until we arrive there." But the Lord hardened Pharoah's heart, and he would not let them go. Then Pharoah said to him, "Get away from me! Take heed to yourself and see my face no more! For the day you see my face you shall die!"

Take your family but leave your goods here in Egypt. It's okay to take your family to church and be a Christian on Sunday but keep your business and all your personal life and practice in Egypt and just go along and get along.

I believe there would have been a compromise Moses could have made that would have satisfied Pharoah, and multitudes of so-called Christians are guilty of this today. Moses says, "Let us go with our family and our goods, and we will send our children back for nine months, each year, to your Egyptian school."

This is the tragic demise of our culture in America. For several generations, we have let the Egyptians train our children in humanist philosophy and take God out of the equation.

Second Compromise

The second compromise of today is a direct result of the first one and will be the ultimate end of our demise. Read Matthew 24:36–39:

But of that day and hour no one knows, not even the angels of heaven, but My Father only. But as the days of Noah *were*, so also will the coming of the Son of Man be. For as in the days before the flood, they were eating and drinking, marrying and giving in marriage, until the day that Noah entered the ark, and did not know until the flood came and took them all away, so also will the coming of the Son of Man be.

Read Genesis 6:1–7:

Now it came to pass, when men began to multiply on the face of the earth and daughters were born to them, the sons of God saw the daughters of men, that they *were* beautiful; and they took wives for themselves of all whom they chose. And the Lord said, "My Spirit shall not strive with man forever, for he is indeed flesh; yet his days shall be one hundred and twenty years." There were giants on the earth in those days and also afterward, when the sons of God came in to the daughters of men and bore *children* to them. Those were mighty men who *were* of old, men of renown. Then the Lord saw that the wickedness of man *was* great in the earth, and *that* every intent of the thoughts of his heart *was* only evil continually. And the Lord was sorry that He had made man on the earth, and He was grieved in His heart. So the Lord said, "I will destroy man whom I have created from the face of the earth, both man and beast, creeping thing and birds of the air, for I am sorry that I have made them."

Read 2 Corinthians 6:14–18, 7:1:

Do not be unequally yoked together with unbelievers. For what fellowship has righteousness with lawlessness? And what communion has light with darkness? And what accord has Christ with Belial? Or what part has a believer with an unbeliever? And what agreement has the temple of God with idols? For you are the temple of the living God. As God as said *"I will dwell in them and walk among them. I will be their God, and they shall be my people."* Therefore, *come out from among them and be separate, says the Lord. Do not touch what is unclean, and I will receive you. I will be a Father to you, and you shall be My sons and daughters, says the Lord Almighty."*

Therefore, having these promises, beloved, let us cleanse ourselves from all filthiness of the flesh and spirit, perfecting holiness in the fear of God.

In Genesis 6, we see the men of the godly line of Seth taking wives of the ungodly line of Cain. As a result, the breakdown of the family and the murders and evil lifestyle of humanity was great upon the earth until the flood came.

Jesus said, "Just as it was in the days of Noah, marrying and giving in marriage." We are there, and I want to close with a bit of godly advice: "Prepare to meet your God."

ABOUT THE AUTHOR

My wife, Ruth, and I have been married for sixty-four years. We have three children, ten grandchildren, and seventeen great-grandchildren. I was raised by an old German family on a dairy farm. They were Lutheran, and I went to a one-room Lutheran school. I was thirty-two years old when I was given a Bible. I, for the first time, read the gospel and was saved and was called to preach. I spent two years in a Bible college while preaching as an evangelist. I soon had planted a new church and school when I met Dr. Jerry Falwell who encouraged me to continue in that direction. My wife and I have planted five churches and three schools and have seen many disciples come through our ministry of over fifty years.